Smart Stud

A Christmas Carol:
Smart Study Guide for GCSE English Literature

Copyright © 2025 Smart Study Press
All rights reserved.
No part of this publication may be reproduced, stored in a retrieval system, or transmitted in any form or by any means-electronic, mechanical, photocopying, recording, or otherwise-without the prior written permission of the publisher, except in the case of brief quotations for educational or review purposes.
This book is a work of educational nonfiction. While every effort has been made to ensure accuracy, neither the author nor the publisher accepts responsibility for any errors or omissions.
ISBN: 9798294547653
First published in the United Kingdom by Smart Study Press

Welcome to Smart Study Press

Smart Study Press exists to make revision clearer, smarter, and more effective. We know how hard it can be to find resources that explain things plainly, match the course you're actually studying, and focus on what really matters in the exam.

This series was designed with one aim in mind: to support students with guides that are genuinely useful. Each book covers exactly what you need to know-nothing more, nothing less-presented in a way that's easy to follow, straightforward to remember, and focused on the skills your exam will reward.

Whether you're starting a topic or revising at the last minute, you'll find clear explanations, structured revision, and practical advice to help you build confidence and improve your results.

Every Smart Study guide follows the same format, so once you've used one, the rest will feel familiar. We'll be expanding the range across subjects and exam boards, but the goal stays the same: to help you revise with clarity, learn what matters most, and give yourself the best possible chance of success.

Thanks for choosing Smart Study Press. Let's get started.

Contents

Welcome to Smart Study Press i

How to Use This Book iv

Chapter 1: The Journey of Scrooge 1

Chapter 2: What Happens and Why It Matters 3

    Chapter 1: Marley's Warning 3

    Chapter 2: The Ghost of Christmas Past 4

    Chapter 3: The Ghost of Christmas Present 5

    Chapter 4: The Ghost of Christmas Yet to Come 6

    Chapter 5: Redemption and Renewal 7

Chapter 3: Key Characters 9

    Ebenezer Scrooge: The Journey of Change 9

    Bob Cratchit: Goodness Under Pressure 11

    Fred: The Spirit of Family and Festivity 12

    Tiny Tim: Hope and Vulnerability 13

    The Spirits: Time, Truth, and Transformation 14

    The Poor and Forgotten: Humanity in the Margins 15

Chapter 4: Important Themes 17

    Redemption: Can People Change? 17

    Responsibility: Who Cares for Whom? 18

    Time: Memory, Action, and Consequence 19

Family and Belonging: Who Is Worth Your Love?..................20

Poverty and Inequality: What Does Society Owe the Poor? 21

Isolation vs Connection: What Does It Mean to Be Alive?..........21

Chapter 5: How Dickens Writes - Language, Form, and Structure .23

Chapter 6: The World Behind the Text 27

Victorian London: A City of Contrasts................................27

The Poor Law and Workhouses.......................................28

Christmas in Victorian England 29

Industrialisation and Inequality 30

Final Thoughts...30

Chapter 7: How to Approach an Essay Question 32

What Will the Question Look Like?.................................33

What the Examiner Is Looking For 34

A Step-by-Step Plan 35

Model Paragraphs...36

Final Takeaway..46

Chapter 8: Why This Text Still Matters................................48

Quick Reference 50

Explore More with Smart Study Press 53

How to Use This Book

This guide is designed to help you revise *A Christmas Carol* with focus and confidence. It won't reteach the whole course - instead, it gives you the essential knowledge, clearly explained and organised in a way that matches how your exam works. Whether you're reading it alongside classroom study or in the run-up to your final assessments, it's here to help you understand key ideas, remember important details, and write stronger responses.

Here's what you'll find:

- Chapter-by-chapter summaries that explain what happens, why it matters, and how it connects to characters, themes, and wider ideas
- Thematic chapters that explore key concepts in depth, using carefully chosen quotations, clear analysis, and contextual insight
- Exam-style tasks and model responses to show you how to apply your knowledge and understand what strong answers look like
- Planning strategies and essay advice to help you build clear, confident responses

- Quick reference tools at the back of the book, bringing together key quotations, terminology, and context links in one place

Most of all, this book is here to support you. Use it in the way that works best for you.

Chapter 1: The Journey of Scrooge

A man sits alone in a cold, dark office. Outside, it's Christmas Eve - snow on the ground, laughter in the streets, warmth in the air. But inside, there is nothing but silence. This is Ebenezer Scrooge - rich, bitter, and utterly alone. He hates the cold, hates the poor, and hates Christmas most of all.

He is about to be haunted.

That night, the ghost of his old business partner appears, dragging heavy chains made from years of greed and selfishness. Marley has come with a warning: change, or suffer the same fate. Scrooge laughs it off. But before the night is over, three more spirits will visit him - one from the past, one from the present, one from the future. Each shows him something he does not want to see. His own life. His own choices. His own end.

That's what makes *A Christmas Carol* one of the most powerful stories ever written. It's not just about ghosts and Christmas. It's about the possibility of change - what happens when someone truly looks at who they are and chooses to be different. Scrooge is not born cruel. But he lets his fear, his greed, and his pain harden him. And unless he changes, he will die unloved and unremembered.

This book is going to take you inside his world. You'll explore the key ideas that run through the story - generosity, regret, family, time, and transformation. You'll meet unforgettable characters like the Cratchits, who have nothing but give everything. You'll see how Dickens uses language to shape emotion, how structure turns one night into a lifetime, and how the novella's historical and political context gave it urgent meaning in Victorian England.

If you're studying for an exam, this book will help you get ready. If you're just reading the story, it will help you understand why it still moves readers today. Either way, get ready - because we are heading into a world of shadows, memory, and hope.

Chapter 2: What Happens and Why It Matters

Dickens didn't call them chapters-he called them staves, like the lines of a song. That's because *A Christmas Carol* isn't just a story. It's meant to feel like music: rising, falling, repeating. Every stave takes us deeper into Scrooge's life and shows us how he changes. What starts as a ghost story becomes something much bigger-a lesson about memory, empathy, and the power of human connection.

This chapter gives you a clear overview of what happens, and just as importantly, why it matters. You'll see how the story builds toward Scrooge's transformation, how key ideas take shape, and how Dickens uses structure to create an emotional journey rather than just a series of events. Keep an eye out for how the past, present, and future work together-not just as plot devices, but as ways of holding Scrooge (and the reader) to account.

Chapter 1: Marley's Warning

The story opens with one simple fact: Marley was dead. Scrooge's old business partner is long gone, but his influence lingers. We meet Scrooge in his office-cold, harsh, and utterly uninterested in human warmth. He refuses to give to charity, turns down his nephew's Christmas invitation, and treats his loyal clerk Bob Cratchit with casual cruelty. He insists that anyone who can't support themselves should simply die and "decrease the surplus population."

But that night, everything begins to shift. Marley's ghost appears, weighed down by chains made from greed, fear, and selfishness. He warns Scrooge that he is heading for the same fate unless he changes-and that three spirits will come to guide him.

Why it matters:

This chapter sets up Scrooge's isolation and emotional deadness. Dickens makes it clear: this man has built his identity on money and rejection, but it has brought him nothing but cold. Marley's warning introduces the theme of consequence and raises a vital question-can a person truly change?

Chapter 2: The Ghost of Christmas Past

The first spirit arrives as a strange, flickering figure-part child, part old man. It shows Scrooge moments from his own early life: a lonely boy in a schoolroom, a warm Christmas with his sister Fan, and a joyful apprenticeship with Mr Fezziwig. But it also shows the moment where everything began to go wrong-when he chose money over love and let his fiancée, Belle, walk away.

Scrooge begins to soften. He tries to argue with the ghost, to block out what he sees. But memory has power. And Scrooge is starting to feel it.

Why it matters:

The past isn't just about nostalgia. It explains who Scrooge became. Dickens uses this chapter to show that cruelty is learned-and so, maybe, it can be unlearned. The ghost also introduces one of the story's key ideas: regret can be painful, but it's the first step to change.

Chapter 3: The Ghost of Christmas Present

This spirit is entirely different-joyful, generous, full of life. It shows Scrooge how other people are spending Christmas: in tiny homes, on distant ships, in the cramped quarters of the Cratchit family. Everywhere it goes, it brings warmth and goodwill. Even those with little to spare are rich in spirit.

At the Cratchit home, Scrooge sees a very different kind of wealth-love, family, and resilience. He's especially moved by Tiny Tim, Bob's disabled son, who is full of kindness and faith despite his illness. "If these shadows remain unaltered by the Future," the spirit warns, "the child will die."

The ghost also shows how Scrooge is perceived-mocked at Fred's house, dismissed by strangers, pitied by those who should fear him. Before vanishing, the spirit reveals two starving children hidden under his robe-Ignorance and Want-and warns that society's cruelty toward the poor will destroy it from within.

Why it matters:

This chapter forces Scrooge to see the world he has ignored. Dickens uses it to expose Victorian inequality and challenge the myth that poverty is a personal failure. The message is clear: you cannot look away from suffering and call yourself human.

Chapter 4: The Ghost of Christmas Yet to Come

The final spirit arrives in silence, draped in black. It shows Scrooge a series of scenes connected by death: businessmen mocking a dead man's funeral, a pawn shop selling off his belongings, a poor family relieved at his passing, and the Cratchits grieving for Tiny Tim.

Eventually, Scrooge realises the dead man is himself.

Faced with this future-alone, unloved, and forgotten-Scrooge finally breaks. He begs for a second chance. "I am not the man I was," he pleads. "Why show me this, if I am past all hope?"

Why it matters:

This is the turning point. The ghost doesn't speak because it doesn't need to. The future is a mirror, and Scrooge cannot look away. Dickens uses this moment to show that fear can be a wake-up call-but the real transformation only comes when fear leads to compassion.

Chapter 5: Redemption and Renewal

Scrooge wakes up on Christmas morning, overjoyed to be alive. He laughs. He dances. He sends a huge turkey to the Cratchits, gives money to charity, and spends the day with Fred's family. The man who once said "Bah! Humbug!" is now overflowing with generosity and warmth.

The story ends with a new kind of legacy. Scrooge becomes "as good a friend, as good a master, and as good a man" as the city has ever known. And Tiny Tim, who did not die, delivers the final line: "God bless us, every one!"

Why it matters:

Scrooge's transformation is complete. But Dickens never lets us forget what it cost to get there. This ending isn't just cheerful-it's a challenge. If Scrooge can change, why can't we? The novella asks every reader to look at their own choices and decide who they want to be.

Chapter 3: Key Characters

What to Know and How to Write About Them

Dickens doesn't waste time easing you in. From the very first page, we are thrown into the emotional and moral centre of the story. This chapter will help you understand each key character's role, development, and significance - and how to write about them in a way that scores marks.

For each major character, we'll explore:

- What makes them important
- How they change (or don't)
- The themes they connect to
- Their key relationships
- Useful quotations

Ebenezer Scrooge: The Journey of Change

Scrooge is the heart of the story - and the character who changes the most. At the beginning, he is cold, greedy, and dismissive of everything human. Dickens uses sharp, sensory language to describe him: "hard and sharp as flint," "solitary as an oyster," "the cold within him froze his old features." These images show not just his emotional isolation but his resistance to change.

Revision Focus: Use "solitary as an oyster" to explore Scrooge's isolation and the possibility of something hidden inside. This metaphor introduces both his harsh shell and his potential to change.

Through his encounters with the three spirits, we see Scrooge go on a journey from detachment to emotional awakening. The past reveals his loneliness and lost love. The present shows him what he's missing - joy, connection, and family. The future confronts him with what his life will mean if nothing changes: death without grief, a name without legacy.

At first, Scrooge resists. But eventually, he breaks. His plea to the final spirit - "I am not the man I was" - marks the turning point. By the end, he is transformed. He laughs, donates, reconnects, and becomes a second father to Tiny Tim.

Revision Focus: Link "I am not the man I was" to the theme of redemption. Dickens presents change not as easy, but as possible - and vital.

Scrooge's arc also drives the novella's message. Dickens uses him to challenge the social cruelty of Victorian England: the idea that poverty is deserved, and that wealth excuses selfishness. In Scrooge, he creates a warning - but also a hope.

Bob Cratchit: Goodness Under Pressure

Bob Cratchit works hard, earns little, and asks for almost nothing. He represents the ordinary poor - kind, patient, and loyal despite unfair treatment. Scrooge underpays him, mocks his needs, and resents giving him Christmas Day off. But Bob never complains. He remains generous and full of love, especially for his family.

Revision Focus: Use Bob's warmth to contrast with Scrooge's coldness. The Cratchit household has little money but emotional richness. This supports exam points about family, poverty, and morality.

Bob's most powerful moments come in how he speaks about Tiny Tim - before and after the vision of his death. He sees value in his child's gentleness and faith, not his usefulness. In Chapter 4, when the spirit shows the Cratchits grieving, Bob's quiet grief gives the story its emotional core.

Revision Focus: Use "he was very light to carry" to explore Bob's tenderness. It highlights how Dickens presents love and grief as sources of dignity, not weakness.

Bob's relationship with Scrooge shifts too. At the end of the novella, Scrooge raises Bob's salary and becomes a kind employer. This moment symbolises more than workplace fairness - it shows the restoration of humanity.

Fred: The Spirit of Family and Festivity

Fred is Scrooge's cheerful nephew - the only family he has, and the only person who openly welcomes him. From the first chapter, Fred represents everything Scrooge rejects: warmth, celebration, generosity, and community.

His speech about Christmas is one of the most important in the novella. He calls it "a good time… when men and women seem by one consent to open their shut-up hearts freely." Unlike Scrooge, Fred sees value in human connection, even when it doesn't profit him financially.

Revision Focus: Fred's voice helps Dickens frame the moral argument of the story. Use his speech to explore themes of celebration, generosity, and the true meaning of Christmas.

Fred also offers forgiveness. Even when mocked, he continues to invite Scrooge, and when Scrooge changes, Fred welcomes him instantly. This is key to the novella's emotional tone: change is always possible, and kindness is never wasted.

Tiny Tim: Hope and Vulnerability

Tiny Tim appears briefly, but powerfully. He is frail, cheerful, and completely unselfish. His famous line - "God bless us, every one!" - becomes the emotional heart of the story. He is not just a symbol of innocence, but of what is at stake if Scrooge fails to change.

Dickens presents Tim as the child of the working poor - vulnerable, dependent on others, and yet full of dignity. When the Ghost of Christmas Present warns that Tim "will die" if nothing changes, it shifts the stakes. Scrooge must act not just for himself, but for the people his choices affect.

Revision Focus: Use Tiny Tim to connect the personal to the political. His fate shows how individual greed (like Scrooge's) contributes to social injustice.

In the future vision, Tiny Tim's death devastates the Cratchits and moves Scrooge to tears. When he wakes, Scrooge's promise to help the family is about more than charity - it's about responsibility and love.

The Spirits: Time, Truth, and Transformation

Each of the three ghosts has a distinct role and mood. They are not just magical plot devices - they represent stages of reflection and growth.

The Ghost of Christmas Past is gentle but firm. It brings memory, regret, and the painful truth of who Scrooge used to be. Its shifting form mirrors the way memory works - flickering, elusive, and emotionally charged.

The Ghost of Christmas Present is joyful and commanding. It embodies generosity and celebration but also challenges injustice. It shows Scrooge what he has ignored and warns of the children Ignorance and Want.

The Ghost of Christmas Yet to Come is silent and terrifying. It reveals Scrooge's potential future and forces him to confront death, isolation, and legacy.

Revision Focus: The spirits are symbolic. Together, they create a structured journey: memory, consequence, and fear. Use them to explore structure, theme, and transformation.

Marley's ghost also plays a crucial role. Unlike the three spirits, Marley is someone Scrooge once trusted - now trapped by the same values Scrooge still lives by. His warning is personal and urgent: "I wear the chain I forged in life." It's not just about fate - it's about choice.

The Poor and Forgotten: Humanity in the Margins

Dickens gives voice to the voiceless through the characters who suffer most: the Cratchits, the carol singer Scrooge scares away, the men collecting for charity, the thieves in the pawnshop. These figures are not just background - they are the moral test of the world Scrooge inhabits.

In a time when poverty was often blamed on the poor themselves, Dickens uses these characters to humanise suffering. He doesn't idealise them - he just shows that they matter. That their lives are full of dignity, fear, effort, and hope.

Revision Focus: Use these characters to strengthen essays on social responsibility. Dickens believed literature could change hearts - and laws.

Chapter 4: Important Themes

On the surface, *A Christmas Carol* is a ghost story. But underneath, it's about how people live, how they treat each other, and what really matters. Dickens wrote the novella not just to entertain, but to challenge his readers - especially the wealthy and powerful - to look at the world around them and ask: what kind of society have we created?

Each theme in the book works on two levels. It shapes the story, and it carries a message. This chapter explores the most important themes and shows how to link them to characters, structure, and context.

Redemption: Can People Change?

Scrooge's journey is a story of moral transformation. At the start, he is cruel and closed-off. By the end, he is generous and joyful. This isn't just a plot device - it's the whole point. Dickens believed that people could change, even if they had lived badly. The key was self-awareness, emotional truth, and a willingness to care.

The ghosts don't force Scrooge to change. They just show him his life. He has to choose. That's what makes his transformation powerful - and believable. It isn't magic. It's recognition.

"I am not the man I was."

Revision Notes: Use this theme in any essay about Scrooge. Tie it to the structure of the novella - each ghost representing a stage in his transformation. Link to the wider idea that Dickens is offering us a chance to change, too.

Responsibility: Who Cares for Whom?

Dickens lived in a time of extreme inequality. Many Victorians believed poverty was the fault of the poor. Dickens disagreed. Through Scrooge, he shows what happens when people stop caring about others - and how dangerous that attitude is.

Scrooge's early views are brutal: "Are there no prisons? Are there no workhouses?" He believes the poor are surplus - a burden to be ignored or punished. By the end, he takes responsibility. Not just for himself, but for Tiny Tim, Bob Cratchit, and the wider world.

"Mankind was my business."

Revision Notes: Use Marley's line to show Dickens' moral message. Tie this theme to the charity collectors, the Cratchits, and the spirit's warning about Ignorance and Want. Good responses will connect this theme to the historical context of the Poor Law and attitudes to poverty.

Time: Memory, Action, and Consequence

The entire story happens in one night - but it spans a lifetime. That's no accident. Dickens uses time not just as a plot device, but as a theme. The ghosts show Scrooge his past, his present, and his future. Together, they force him to see time as connected: what you do now affects what comes next.

Scrooge's problem is that he has stopped thinking in human time. He hoards money as if he will live forever. The spirits make him realise: life is short. There is still time to change - but only if he acts now.

> *"No space of regret can make amends for one life's opportunity misused."*

Revision Notes: Use this theme in essays about structure or the ghosts. Link it to Scrooge's obsession with money - and how he has lost touch with emotional time (seasons, family rituals, growing up, ageing). Strong responses will show how Dickens uses time to give the story urgency.

Family and Belonging: Who Is Worth Your Love?

Scrooge has money, but no one to love. He rejects his nephew Fred, cuts himself off from memory, and ends up alone in a grave no one visits. In contrast, the Cratchits have almost nothing - but they are rich in connection.

Dickens presents family not as perfect, but as necessary. Fred's love is unwavering. The Cratchits are chaotic and cramped, but full of laughter. Even Scrooge's memories - his sister Fan, his lost fiancée Belle - show that belonging matters more than wealth.

> *"A solitary child, neglected by his friends."*

Revision Notes: Use this theme to link characters. Scrooge begins alone but ends connected. Tie it to the theme of change - family is one of the forces that brings him back to himself. You can also use it to contrast characters: Fred vs. Scrooge, or Cratchit family vs. Scrooge's loneliness.

Poverty and Inequality: What Does Society Owe the Poor?

Dickens makes the social message of *A Christmas Carol* impossible to ignore. He gives names, faces, and emotions to the poor - and shows how easy it is for the rich to look away. Scrooge's dismissal of the poor early in the story is presented as inhuman. His transformation is not complete until he understands the need for generosity.

The Cratchits symbolise dignity in hardship. Tiny Tim becomes the emotional centre of the story. And the two children beneath the Ghost of Christmas Present - Ignorance and Want - are a warning: if society keeps ignoring the poor, it will collapse.

> *"This boy is Ignorance. This girl is Want. Beware them both."*

Revision Notes: Use this theme in essays about the novella's purpose or context. Tie it to Dickens' own life and his critique of the Poor Law. Strong responses show that Dickens isn't just asking Scrooge to change - he's asking all of us.

Isolation vs Connection: What Does It Mean to Be Alive?

At its core, this is a story about emotional life. Scrooge begins as the embodiment of isolation - walled off from love, family, and compassion. He believes relationships are a waste. But the ghosts show him that disconnection is a kind of death.

By the end, Scrooge reconnects - to others and to himself. His transformation is not just moral, but emotional. He opens his heart.

"He became as good a friend, as good a master, and as good a man."

Revision Notes: Use this theme to explore mood and character. Scrooge's change isn't about saying the right things - it's about feeling again. Tie this to Dickens' use of setting (cold vs warmth, light vs dark) and to the structure of the story as a journey from emotional death to life.

Chapter 5: How Dickens Writes - Language, Form, and Structure

Understanding *how* Dickens tells his story is just as important as knowing *what* happens. In *A Christmas Carol*, language, narrative form, and structure work together to create a powerful and memorable experience that brings Dickens's themes and characters to life.

Here are the key ways Dickens achieves this:

- Vivid, symbolic language that reveals character and mood
- A ghost story structure that frames the narrative and adds urgency
- Careful emotional pacing that builds tension to a powerful climax
- Accessible style balanced with humour and social critique

Dickens's language is vivid and carefully chosen to create mood and reveal character. Early on, Scrooge is described as "hard and sharp as flint" and "solitary as an oyster." These metaphors highlight his coldness and isolation while also suggesting a hidden potential for change beneath his tough exterior. The repeated phrase "Bah! Humbug!" captures his dismissive, bitter attitude toward Christmas and generosity, marking him as emotionally closed off. Names like Tiny Tim carry symbolic weight - Tim's smallness and innocence make him a powerful figure of vulnerability and hope. Dickens also uses direct speech to great effect: Fred's cheerful greeting, "A merry Christmas, uncle! God save you!" contrasts sharply with Scrooge's gruff response, highlighting their opposing attitudes. Similarly, Bob Cratchit's gentle, "My little, little child!" invites sympathy and highlights the warmth of family amidst hardship.

Revision Notes: When writing about language, support your points with specific quotations and explain how Dickens's word choices create mood or reveal character.

The ghost story form frames the entire narrative and is central to its effect. The visits from the three spirits move Scrooge-and readers-through past, present, and future, allowing reflection on memory, consequence, and possibility. For example, the Ghost of Christmas Past's "strange figure-like a child and like an old man" with a "bright clear jet of light" symbolises memory's flickering and sometimes painful nature. The Ghost of Christmas Present's "jolly giant" appearance, surrounded by food and laughter, contrasts with the Ghost of Christmas Yet to Come's silent, dark figure, cloaked and mysterious, embodying fear of death and the unknown. This clear narrative structure adds urgency and drama, with each ghost representing a different stage of Scrooge's moral journey. It also allows Dickens to combine entertainment with a serious social message, making the story both engaging and instructive.

Revision Notes: Link the ghost story form to the novella's themes. Show how the spirits represent stages of Scrooge's transformation and create dramatic tension.

Structurally, Dickens carefully builds emotional tension throughout the novella. Each ghost reveals more about Scrooge's life and mistakes, escalating the stakes. The vision of Scrooge's lonely death- the silent graveyard scene where "the spirit did not answer, but pointed onward"-is the emotional climax: chilling and powerful, it forces both Scrooge and readers to confront the consequences of a life without compassion. The final chapter offers resolution and hope, showing that redemption is possible and that generosity can transform even the hardest heart. Scrooge's joyful exclamation, "I will live in the Past, the Present, and the Future!" signals his complete transformation.

Revision Notes: Discuss how Dickens controls the reader's emotions through structure-building tension to a climax, then providing catharsis and hope.

Dickens's accessible style helps the novella reach a wide audience, combining clear language with moments of humour and satire. Fred's playful teasing-"What reason have you to be merry? You're poor enough"-balances the critique with warmth and invites readers to reconsider their assumptions. Meanwhile, Dickens's emotional appeals invite readers to sympathise with the poor and reconsider societal attitudes toward poverty and responsibility. The figures of Ignorance and Want, described as "wretched, abject, frightful, hideous, miserable," starkly warn of society's neglect.

Revision Notes: Consider how Dickens's tone-mixing humour and emotional appeal-makes his social critique more persuasive and engaging.

When writing about *A Christmas Carol*, it is important to consider not just what Dickens shows but how he shows it. The careful choice of language, the ghost story form, and the rising emotional structure all work together to support the novella's themes and message.

Revision Notes: Always link your analysis of language, form, and structure back to the novella's themes and characters to show a full understanding

Chapter 6: The World Behind the Text

Understanding *A Christmas Carol* fully means stepping back from the story and looking at the world Dickens lived in. The Victorian era was a time of massive change and great inequality. Dickens wrote the novella not just as a ghost story, but as a response to the social problems he saw all around him.

Victorian London: A City of Contrasts

Dickens knew London better than most. It was the largest city in the world, full of energy and opportunity - but also overcrowded, filthy, and dangerous. Wealth and poverty existed side by side: grand mansions next to slums where families lived in tiny, cramped rooms.

This setting shapes the story. Scrooge's office and home feel cold and lonely, while the Cratchit house, though poor, is full of warmth and life. Dickens wanted readers to see these contrasts clearly - to recognise that poverty was not just about money but about social isolation.

Revision Notes: Use the contrasting settings in essays to show how Dickens highlights social division and the emotional impact of poverty.

The Poor Law and Workhouses

In 1834, the Poor Law Amendment Act changed how Britain cared for the poor. It made help conditional on entering workhouses, which were harsh, prison-like places. Many people feared and hated workhouses because families were separated and conditions were terrible.

Scrooge's early views echo this attitude when he asks, "Are there no prisons? Are there no workhouses?" This reflects a common belief among the wealthy that poverty was the fault of the poor - that they were lazy or undeserving.

Dickens himself was a critic of the Poor Law. Through *A Christmas Carol*, he challenged readers to reject this cruelty and see the humanity in everyone.

Revision Notes: Reference the Poor Law to explain the social critique in the novella and Scrooge's initial attitudes toward the poor.

Christmas in Victorian England

During Dickens's era, Christmas Day was a public holiday in England, but for many people it lacked the special significance it holds today. In industrial cities and working-class communities, it was common for people to work on Christmas or have only brief time off. The familiar traditions of festive feasting, gift-giving, and family gatherings were just starting to develop.

Dickens's *A Christmas Carol* played a major role in shaping this transformation. His vivid portrayal of generosity, celebration, and community helped popularise the idea of Christmas as a time for kindness and togetherness. Through scenes like Fred's joyful invitation to his uncle and the Cratchit family's humble but heartfelt feast, Dickens captured and encouraged the spirit of a holiday that continues to resonate with readers and shape modern celebrations.

Revision Notes: Use the historical context of Christmas celebrations to deepen analysis of the novella's festive scenes and their symbolic meaning.

Industrialisation and Inequality

The Industrial Revolution brought great wealth to some but left many behind. Factories and new technologies changed how people lived and worked, often worsening conditions for the poor.

Dickens was deeply aware of this gap. The characters of Ignorance and Want under the Ghost of Christmas Present are a clear warning about the dangers of ignoring social injustice. Dickens's novella urges readers to care for those left behind by progress.

Revision Notes: Link the Industrial Revolution context to the social message of the novella, especially through the symbols of Ignorance and Want.

Final Thoughts

A Christmas Carol remains one of the most powerful stories about human kindness and change. Dickens's vivid characters, haunting ghosts, and urgent social message continue to inspire readers to reflect on their own choices. As you study the novella, remember that its heart lies in the possibility of transformation-not just for Scrooge, but for all of us.

Revision Tip: Use this chapter to add depth to essays. Linking the novella's social message to Victorian context shows strong understanding. Don't just focus on the story - explain why Dickens wrote it and what he hoped to achieve.

Chapter 7: How to Approach an Essay Question

Revision is about preparing to show off what you know - not catching you out.

An exam isn't a trap set by a cruel examiner. It's your chance to take control of the conversation. You're not being asked to guess what's in the examiner's head - you're being invited to show what's in yours. And if you've put in the work, this is your moment to shine.

Literature isn't just about remembering what happens. It's about understanding how and why it happens - how a writer like Dickens uses language, structure, and character to explore huge ideas like generosity, responsibility, change, and social justice. The examiner wants to see that you can think clearly, notice details, and explain your ideas with confidence.

That means this isn't about sounding clever or using fancy words. It's about building a strong, clear argument that shows you know the novella from the inside out. Think of the essay as a performance: you're walking onstage, spotlight on, ready to show what you can do. This chapter will help you rehearse for that moment - step by step.

What Will the Question Look Like?

GCSE questions on *A Christmas Carol* usually follow a familiar pattern. You'll be given a short extract from the novella and a prompt asking you to explore how Dickens presents a particular theme or character. For example, you might see:

> "Starting with this extract, explore how Dickens presents generosity in *A Christmas Carol*."

At heart, these questions ask you to do three things. First, zoom in on the extract. How does Dickens use language, structure, and tone to shape meaning in this moment? Second, zoom out to the wider novella. How does this scene connect to characters, themes, or events elsewhere? And third, connect to context. How might a Victorian audience have understood the ideas in this scene - especially around charity, poverty, or family?

Think of your essay as a triangle: extract, novella, context. The strongest responses move confidently between these three points, showing not just what happens, but how Dickens shapes it and why it mattered then - and still matters now.

What the Examiner Is Looking For

Behind every question is a clear set of expectations. The examiner wants to see that you understand the novella as a crafted piece of writing - one that uses language and structure to explore powerful ideas. A top-level essay will do three key things:

Make a clear, thoughtful argument that answers the question

- Zoom in on Dickens's language and structure to show how meaning is created
- Link ideas to the wider novella and its context, especially how a Victorian audience might respond
- These are the core skills being assessed - no matter your exam board.

The best essays do this in four main ways:

First, they present a clear, consistent argument. Every paragraph builds on the one before and keeps coming back to the question. Second, they zoom in on Dickens's choices - his imagery, structure, tone, and characterisation - and link them to meaning.

Third, they make links across the novella: echoing earlier scenes or foreshadowing what's to come. Finally, they use context where it deepens understanding - not as a list of facts, but as part of the emotional and social world of the story.

A Step-by-Step Plan

1. Read the Question Carefully: Underline the key theme or character. Make sure you know what the question really asks - and stay focused on that idea throughout.
2. Read the Extract with Focus: Don't just read for meaning. Notice the tone. Pay attention to how the character speaks. Look for imagery, metaphors, and any shifts in mood or direction.
3. Plan Three Main Ideas: Before writing, decide on three strong points to make. These might include a shift in character, a repeated image, or a contrast between characters or ideas.
4. Build Analytical Paragraphs: Use a flexible Point-Evidence-Explain-Link structure. Don't just spot a technique - unpack what it does. For example:

Dickens describes Scrooge as "a squeezing, wrenching, grasping, scraping, clutching, covetous old sinner."

The repetition of harsh verbs creates a rhythm of cruelty and greed, emphasising how utterly selfish Scrooge has become. This language makes Scrooge's transformation later in the novella even more powerful.

5. Zoom Out to the Whole Novella: Ask how this moment connects to other scenes. Does the theme develop or shift later? Are there characters who echo or challenge this idea? Show you're thinking beyond the extract.
6. Bring in Context Thoughtfully: Only use historical or social references that support your point. If you're writing about poverty or charity, think about how Victorian audiences would have responded - and why that matters.
7. Finish Clearly: Your conclusion doesn't need to be long but should tie your ideas together and show you've answered the question clearly and thoughtfully.

Model Paragraphs

Below are example paragraphs responding to typical *A Christmas Carol* questions. These are not full essays but show strong responses demonstrating the key skills: making a clear point, zooming in on language and structure, linking to the wider novella, and using context where it deepens meaning.

Use these as guides to the shape, detail, and style expected. Try practising by completing them or writing your own paragraphs.

Example Question 1:

Starting with this extract, explore how Dickens presents Scrooge's attitude towards Christmas.

"Bah! Humbug!"

The phrase "Bah! Humbug!" instantly defines Scrooge's dismissive and cynical attitude towards Christmas. The short, guttural interjection "Bah!" conveys irritation, while "Humbug" implies that he sees Christmas as a deceit or fraud - something fake, sentimental, and undeserving of celebration. Dickens uses this phrase not just as a catchphrase, but as a window into Scrooge's worldview: closed-off, joyless, and deeply mistrustful of emotional generosity.

This attitude is reinforced throughout Stave 1. Scrooge rejects charitable appeals, sneers at his nephew Fred's festive cheer, and grudgingly allows his clerk a single day off. Dickens builds a portrait of a man who sees no value in human connection. His office is described as cold and dark, reflecting both his environment and his inner life. Even the weather seems scared to affect him - he is emotionally frozen, untouched by the warmth that Christmas represents.

Crucially, Dickens doesn't just present Scrooge as mean-spirited for no reason. Instead, he shows us the consequences of choosing self-interest over empathy. By making Scrooge so extreme in his rejection of Christmas, Dickens sets up the dramatic arc of transformation. The more hostile and emotionally starved Scrooge appears at the beginning, the more powerful his eventual change will feel.

Victorian readers would have recognised Scrooge's attitude as not only unkind but dangerously out of step with Christian and social values. Christmas, for Dickens, is not just a holiday - it is a symbol of compassion, community, and second chances. Scrooge's contempt for it represents a deeper moral failure: the refusal to see others as part of one shared human family.

By the end of the novella, Scrooge's transformation is defined by the reversal of this initial stance. He becomes "as good a friend, as good a master, and as good a man as the good old city knew." His rediscovery of Christmas is symbolic of his rediscovery of human feeling. That makes "Bah! Humbug!" more than just a grumpy phrase - it becomes a marker of everything Scrooge must unlearn in order to become fully human again.

In sum, Dickens presents Scrooge's attitude towards Christmas as cold, dismissive, and rooted in emotional isolation. Through language, characterisation, and contrast, he sets up a powerful transformation - one that invites readers to consider not just how we celebrate Christmas, but how we treat others all year round.

Examiner's Comments:

This is a really strong sample paragraph that shows the kind of insight and precision needed for top-level responses. You've started with a clear focus on the question and built a thoughtful analysis of the phrase "Bah! Humbug!" - not just explaining what it means, but exploring how Dickens uses it to reveal Scrooge's worldview. The way you link Scrooge's language to his emotional isolation and connect that to the symbolic setting (the cold, dark office) is especially effective. There's also excellent awareness of how Dickens uses Scrooge's early attitude to prepare the reader for his transformation later in the novella. These big-picture ideas are exactly what examiners look for at the top end.

Because this is just a single paragraph, there are naturally some things that would need developing in a full essay. For example, in a complete response you'd want to include more specific quotation evidence - perhaps from Scrooge's conversations with Fred or the charity collectors - to show how his rejection of Christmas is expressed in different ways. You could also build in more detail about how Dickens uses contrast across the whole structure of the novella, especially between Stave 1 and Stave 5. A top-level answer often tracks changes in tone, so exploring the shift from cold detachment to joyful generosity would help deepen your analysis of Scrooge's development.

So overall, this paragraph is a really strong foundation: it shows clear understanding of the text, confident use of context, and some thoughtful language and structural analysis. To turn it into a full top-grade essay, you'd just need to expand on these ideas with more examples, closer textual detail, and a clearer sense of how Dickens develops Scrooge's attitude across the whole novella. Keep going - you're on the right track.

Example Question 2:

Starting with this extract, explore how Dickens presents the Cratchit family.

"My little, little child!"

In this extract, Bob Cratchit's repetition of "little" shows the depth of his grief and love for Tiny Tim. The simple, broken rhythm of "My little, little child!" captures his devastation - not through dramatic action, but through quiet, heartfelt sorrow. Dickens uses this moment to show the emotional richness of the Cratchit family. Although they are poor in material terms, they are rich in love, care, and dignity.

Throughout A Christmas Carol, Dickens uses the Cratchits as a moral contrast to Scrooge. They are warm where he is cold, generous where he is selfish, and emotionally connected where he is isolated. Their Christmas dinner scene is full of joy and humour despite its modesty, showing that happiness is not about wealth but about shared humanity. Dickens carefully constructs this family as an ideal of working-class virtue - not because they are perfect, but because they care for each other deeply.

The use of Tiny Tim as a symbolic figure intensifies the reader's emotional connection. His famous line "God bless us, every one!" represents innocence, generosity, and hope - values that Scrooge has rejected. Tim's death in the alternate future serves as a warning: without social responsibility and change, the vulnerable will suffer. Bob's grief is not just personal - it stands for all poor families struggling in a system that ignores them.

Dickens's portrayal of the Cratchits is not politically neutral. He wanted readers to see the humanity of the working poor, especially at a time when the Poor Law and workhouse system treated poverty as a moral failing. By giving the Cratchits humour, pride, and emotional depth, he challenges the dehumanising attitudes of Victorian society. The Cratchits are not passive victims - they are active symbols of what family and love should look like.

For a Victorian reader, this portrayal would have been moving and provocative. Dickens was writing during a time of intense social inequality, and A Christmas Carol was part of a wider campaign for reform. He wanted the middle and upper classes to see the poor not as statistics, but as people - with names, feelings, and families. The Cratchits make that idea real.

In sum, Dickens presents the Cratchit family as a model of warmth, love, and emotional integrity. Through their joy and sorrow, he contrasts them with Scrooge's isolation and challenges readers to recognise the moral cost of ignoring those in need. The line "My little, little child!" is a moment of raw feeling - but it also echoes the novella's larger message: we are all connected, and we all have a duty to care.

Examiner's Comments:

This is a strong and insightful revision paragraph that shows clear understanding of how Dickens presents the Cratchit family. The analysis of "My little, little child!" is thoughtful, especially the comment on broken rhythm to convey grief, and you link this effectively to Dickens's broader message about emotional richness and human dignity. The paragraph also shows confident awareness of context, particularly in highlighting Dickens's critique of Victorian attitudes toward poverty and the Poor Law. To develop this into a full high-level essay, you'd need to include a wider range of textual moments - such as the Christmas dinner scene or the Ghost of Christmas Present's warning - and explore how the Cratchits are used structurally across the novella. A deeper look at contrast with other families or how Dickens builds their portrayal over time would also strengthen the response. As a single paragraph, this is a strong foundation - with more textual evidence and development, it could form part of a top-grade answer..

Example Question 3:

Starting with this extract, explore how Dickens presents Tiny Tim.

"God bless us, every one!"

Tiny Tim's line "God bless us, every one!" encapsulates his role as a symbol of innocence, generosity, and moral clarity. The inclusive pronoun "us" expands the blessing beyond his own family, offering kindness to all, regardless of wealth or status. The phrase is strikingly simple, yet emotionally powerful - its repetition throughout the novella gives it weight, suggesting that Tim's voice, though small, carries great significance.

Dickens presents Tiny Tim as a child who, despite poverty and illness, radiates compassion. His physical frailty is contrasted with his emotional strength: he does not express bitterness, but hope. The Cratchits' love for him, particularly Bob's tender repetition of "My little, little child" after his imagined death, reinforces the emotional value placed on Tim's life. In doing so, Dickens makes Tim the moral centre of the novella - the character whose fate most clearly reveals the consequences of Scrooge's choices.

Importantly, Tiny Tim is not just a character - he is a symbol. For a Victorian audience, he would have represented the real suffering of poor children in industrial Britain. Dickens, a committed social reformer, uses Tim to elicit empathy and urge change. His potential death, revealed by the Ghost of Christmas Yet to Come, is not just personal tragedy but social indictment. The message is clear: if the wealthy ignore the suffering of the vulnerable, they become complicit in it.

By placing "God bless us, every one!" at the Cratchits' Christmas dinner - a moment of joy in a life of hardship - Dickens contrasts material poverty with emotional richness. The Cratchits may have little, but they value love, unity, and generosity. This reflects the novella's broader theme: that true wealth lies not in money but in human connection.

Tiny Tim's ultimate survival at the end of the story symbolises the positive impact of Scrooge's transformation. When Scrooge chooses compassion, it quite literally saves lives. That gives Tim's blessing retroactive power - not just a pious hope, but a vision of what can be. Through this small, gentle voice, Dickens delivers one of the novella's largest messages: that every life matters, and even the weakest among us can carry the greatest wisdom.

In sum, Dickens presents Tiny Tim as the embodiment of moral goodness, emotional clarity, and redemptive possibility. His presence in the novella is brief, but his significance is immense - a reminder that the measure of a society lies in how it treats its most vulnerable.

Examiner's Comments:

This is a thoughtful and well-crafted paragraph that shows a strong understanding of how Dickens uses Tiny Tim as both character and symbol. The analysis of the line "God bless us, every one!" is especially effective, with clear attention to language and its symbolic weight across the novella. You've also made excellent links to wider themes, particularly the contrast between material poverty and emotional richness, and you handle the historical context with maturity, recognising how Dickens used Tim to challenge Victorian attitudes to poverty. To develop this into a full essay, you would need to explore a wider range of textual references - for example, the Ghost of Christmas Present's commentary on Tim, or how Scrooge reacts to hearing Tim's name at the end. Some deeper structural insight - such as how Dickens places Tim's imagined death at a turning point in Scrooge's journey - would also help show how Tim's role functions across the whole narrative. As a single paragraph, this is a strong foundation for a high-level answer; building out your analysis across more of the text would help meet the full demands of a top-grade response.

Final Takeaway

Make a clear argument, support it with precise analysis, and show how the moment fits the whole novella. Every sentence should help answer the question.

Remember, the goal isn't to memorise examples but to understand the method behind them. Each paragraph models how to build a strong argument: start with a clear point, support it with evidence, then explain how Dickens's choices affect meaning, character, and audience response. The tone should be confident but accessible.

Use these examples as a springboard. Ask yourself: what makes this work? What choices has Dickens made? Then try writing your own versions. The more you practise, the more confident you'll be in the exam.

Think clearly. Write simply. Show what you know.

Chapter 8: Why This Text Still Matters

Even though it was written nearly two hundred years ago, *A Christmas Carol* still speaks powerfully to modern audiences. The language may feel old-fashioned at times, but the questions it asks are as urgent now as they were then.

What happens when we ignore the needs of others? How can kindness and generosity transform a person - and a society? What responsibility do we have to those who are vulnerable? How do our choices ripple beyond ourselves?

These are human questions, not just Victorian ones. We still see communities struggling with inequality and poverty. We still debate how much we owe to each other - as individuals, as neighbours, and as a society. We still face the challenge of opening our hearts in a world that can be cold and isolating.

This is also a story about change and hope. Dickens's characters are more than symbols - they are deeply human, flawed, and capable of growth. That is part of what makes the novella so powerful. It doesn't just tell us what people do; it shows us how compassion can heal and transform.

For all its ghosts and supernatural visits, the real magic of the story lies in its call to empathy and action. Scrooge's journey reminds us that it is never too late to change, to care, and to make a difference.

Studying this text is not just about passing exams. It's about learning to see the world with kindness, to ask difficult questions, and to understand the impact of our choices - personal and political.

That is why *A Christmas Carol* still matters.

Quick Reference

Use this section in the final days before your exam. It brings together the most useful ideas, quotes, and terms to keep fresh in your mind.

Key Quotations by Theme

Generosity and Compassion

- "God bless us, every one!" - Tiny Tim's inclusive blessing symbolises hope and kindness
- "If they would rather die, they had better do it, and decrease the surplus population." - Scrooge's harsh view of the poor at the start
- "I will honour Christmas in my heart, and try to keep it all the year." - Scrooge's promise of transformation

Social Responsibility and Poverty

- "Are there no prisons? Are there no workhouses?" - Scrooge's callous attitude toward poverty
- "This boy is Ignorance. This girl is Want." - The Ghost of Christmas Present's warning about social neglect
- "A squeezing, wrenching, grasping, scraping, clutching, covetous old sinner!" - Description of Scrooge's greed

Change and Redemption

- "I am not the man I was." - Scrooge's plea to the Ghost of Christmas Yet to Come

- "Darkness is cheap, and Scrooge liked it." - His preference for isolation and miserliness before change
- "I will live in the Past, the Present, and the Future!" - Scrooge's joyful embrace of life and generosity

Family and Community

- "My little, little child!" - Bob Cratchit's love for Tiny Tim
- "A merry Christmas, uncle! God save you!" - Fred's warm invitation
- "There is nothing in the world so irresistibly contagious as laughter and good humour." - The spirit of Christmas joy

Useful Terminology

Symbolism - Using objects or characters to represent bigger ideas (e.g., Tiny Tim symbolising innocence and hope)

Repetition - Repeating words or phrases to emphasise meaning (e.g., "Bah! Humbug!")

Contrast - Placing opposing ideas side by side (e.g., Scrooge's coldness vs. Cratchit family warmth)

Foreshadowing - Clues about what will happen later (e.g., Marley's chains symbolising consequences)

Narrative structure - How the story is organised, especially the ghost visits showing past, present, and future

Tone - The attitude or mood created by the writer's language (e.g., harsh, joyful, hopeful)

Key Context Links

Victorian social issues - Extreme poverty, Poor Law workhouses, and growing awareness of social responsibility

Christmas traditions - How Dickens helped shape the modern festive season focused on family, charity, and goodwill

Industrial Revolution - The era's economic changes increased wealth for some but hardship for many others

Christian morality - Themes of forgiveness, charity, and redemption reflecting Victorian values

Dickens's own experiences - His childhood poverty and work in a blacking factory influenced his social concerns

Explore More with Smart Study Press

If you found this guide helpful, check out the full Smart Study Press series. Each book is designed to help you revise with clarity, confidence, and exam focus.

We publish expert revision guides for:

- English Literature - including Macbeth, An Inspector Calls, *A Christmas Carol*, Poetry Anthologies, and more
- History - including Elizabethan England, Germany 1890-1945, America 1920-1973, The Norman Conquest, and others
- Geography - including Natural Hazards, Urban Issues, Global Development, and Physical Landscapes in the UK
- Religious Studies - covering key beliefs and ethical topics such as Peace and Conflict, Crime and Punishment, and Human Rights
- Citizenship - exploring UK society, politics, and themes like Democracy, Rights and Responsibilities, and Active Citizenship

Search Smart Study Press on Amazon to see the full range.

If this guide helped, please consider leaving a review - it supports others and helps us keep making great resources.

Printed in Dunstable, United Kingdom